FROM THE MAROONS TO MARCUS

A HISTORICAL DEVELOPMENT

FROM THE MAROONS TO MARCUS

TO MARCUS

A HISTORICAL DEVELOPMENT

SEKOU TAFARI

ILLUSTRATIONS BY KEITH LOVELACE

INTRODUCTION BY W. W. HISLOP

Livicated to all the free children of the Caribbean working people; and for those Africans who fought against chattel slavery, and to those of us who must continue the fight against industrial slavery.

Sekou Tafari

A special Livication to Makeba and Malika along with Brother Samora and all the other children of the Caribbean.

1st published by Research Associates, School Times Publications,
8 Green Gables Park, Meade St., Ext. Eldorado, Tunapuna, Trinidad, W.I.

1st Printing 1985
2nd Reprint Spring 1986 – London
3rd Edition – Updated & Revised 1987

1st US Edition – 1990
2nd US Edition – 2004

Library of Congress Catalogue Number 89-63799

ISBN: 0-948392-00x

Published by FRONTLINE BOOKS
751 E 75th Street, Chicago, Illinois 60619

Illustrations: Keith Lovelace

NEW PUBLICATIONS

1) **Rasta: Halle Sellassie & the Rastafarians**
2) **The Mission**
3) **The Royal Parchment Scroll of Black Supremacy**
4) **From the Maroons to Marcus – A historical Development**
   By Sekou Tafari
5) **The Holy Piby AKA The Black Man's Bible**
6) **The Groundings With My Brother** – Walter Rodney (US Edition)

**Research Associates School Times Publications
Caribbean, London, USA.**

INTRODUCTION

To understand Marcus Moziah Garvey, it is extremely important to study the mood, behaviour, development and prejudices of the people of the time. The time was the beginning of the twentieth century. Slavery had only come to an end in 1834.

In the United States, the Africans were struggling in every area of economic and social endeavours in their search for an identity. The names of many Africans who had fought for the emancipation from slavery were remembered only by those who were brave and intelligent enough to announce the achievements of these heroes.

The West Indies were the properties of various European powers and the African citizens were regarded as a means of production.

It was not difficult therefore for any African to dislike the system which governed his life, for the atrocious and inhuman treatment that were experienced were commonplace. Then too, any such race of people who has had their destiny set by another race of people must have developed a feeling of inferiority complex and vice versa.

The legislation in many of the British Territories favoured Europeans and this was not so only in the West Indies, but anywhere where Africans were the labour power. The situation in Jamaica, the birthplace of Garvey, was one where few persons voiced their disapproval of the system. History shows many savage treatments that Blacks suffered under, in their efforts to bring attention to the authorities concerning the inequalities in the System. People became afraid to voice their feelings.

As religious associations were guaranteed under the British and American constitutions, the Africans formed churches in which they gathered in large groups to pray and express their disappointments. Many Africans became members by their oratory, many earned the position of leaders and championed the causes of others.

Marcus Moziah Garvey appeared as an African who had been born and educated in Jamaica. He grew up in a world where Africans were denied their basic human rights and as Garvey puts it "they did not have a place of their own".

His travels to the United States brought him face to face with racial discrimination. This he believed was partly owing to the fact that Blacks were too scattered in the diaspora. To alleviate the problem, Garvey organised the "Back to Africa" Movement and with the help of his newspaper he sent the call out to all Africans. His concept was opposed by other Africans but when his organisation became universal, many changed their opinions about his views.

The thought and opinions of Marcus Moziah Garvey must not be left dormant. His contribution awoke in millions of people, a consciousness and gave them a purpose to live. The teaching of his works is of paramount importance nowadays. Students must not, however, try to live in the past, but use the movement, methods and dedication of Moziah Garvey to give them strength in their struggles to bring about a more humane society for the good of all.

Wilbur W. Hislop

Wilbur W. Hislop
Belmont Junior Secondary
Social Studies

The Rt Hon Marcus Moziah Garvey

YOU HAVE AFRICA, you are in other continents and the islands of the sea, you are millions upon millions strong. I appeal to you stop being the under-dogs and footstools of others, stop complaining, whining and talking about bad luck and misfortune — Shake yourself — get up — start over, overcome the ills around you, you are responsible for what you are, what you want to be, blame no one but yourself, you have the chance, what you want is the will to do, and to dare others to stop you. This is my hope for you and this is the fear others have for you. That is why they watch you so carefully — that you may not get away with any progressive ideas which would be a surprise to the world of theirs.
Marcus Mosiah Garvey 1887-1940

JAMAICA — EARLY COLONIAL HISTORY

JAMAICA or Xaymaca, as the Amerindians used to call it, is about 11,424 sq km in size. Columbus arrived in Jamaica in 1494. He called the island Sant Jago, but it has maintained its original Indian name — Jamaica. Jamaica, as the other Caribbean islands was also a slave colony. Slavery started in Jamaica as early as 1517, when the first Africans were brought there by the Spanish Colonialists from Angola, although the Spaniards had taken control of the island since 1509.

The slaves who followed came from West African countries such as Ghana, Nigeria and the Ivory Coast.

THE BRITISH UNDER CROMWELL

IN 1655, Oliver Cromwell was ruling Britain, and he sent in his troops under Admirals Venables and Penn to invade the island. The British troops consisted of mercenaries, regular soldiers, privateers and pirates.

The British troops fought a fierce battle against the island's then Colonist — the Spaniards. It took the British force five years before the Spanish resistance ended in 1660.

THE EMERGENCE OF THE MAROONS

AFTER the invasion, the Spaniards abandoned their slaves. Some of these slaves then migrated into the hilly eastern mountainous region; and into the Cockpit country, where they organised themselves into a tribal community for cultural and spiritual purposes; and also for defending themselves against attacks by the colonists.

THE MAROONS

FROM around 1662, the runaway or escaped slaves were called Maroons. The Maroons became well known for raiding slave plantations and freeing slaves while encouraging them to join their independent settlement.

The Maroons were brave African men, women and children who loved and upheld freedom more than anything else in the world.

These escaped slaves or freedom fighters never saw Jamaica as their home, but in fact always saw their homeland as Africa — that vast rich continent from where they were forcibly removed.

In the Cockpit country the Maroons practised their own tribal customs, similar to what were practised in Africa. Their settlements were collectively organised around chiefs; and they continued their various spiritual and cultural ceremonial beliefs uninterrupted. Example, they sang tribal songs and played the drums.

The Maroons were fearless fighters, and they never forgave the colonialists for introducing them to that brutal and barbaric institution called slavery.

CUDJOE — THE MOUNTAIN LION

ONE of the most famous Maroons was a man called Cudjoe. Cudjoe was also called by the alias — the Mountain Lion. Cudjoe was born in 1678. He had escaped after the British had quelled a slave revolt in 1690. On escaping he joined the ranks of the runaway slaves. He later became the warchief of the Maroons.

ABOLISHMENT OF SLAVERY

SLAVERY was officially abolished in Jamaica and other English controlled Caribbean islands on August 1st, 1834, but due to the apprenticeship period which was between four and seven years, most slaves really became free men and women in 1838.

THE BIRTH OF GARVEY

ON the 17th of August 1887, a beautiful young African man-child was born in St Ann's Bay, Jamaica. This young man was named Marcus Moziah Garvey. His father, whose name was also Marcus, was a Stonemason by trade, and a strong descendant of the Maroon tribesmen.

GARVEY'S EARLY YEARS

GARVEY'S education was average. He didn't attend Secondary School, but had access to a vast amount of reading materials from his father's library, and later from his Printing tutor, Mr Burrows, from whom he learnt the printing trade.

When young Marcus was only fifteen years old, he left for Kingston.

After a few years in Kingston, Garvey became involved in the art of Journalism. He used Journalism as a form to express the problems of the poor black man, and to educate and inform the people about world issues. He published his first newspaper — Garvey's Watchman — sometime around 1910.

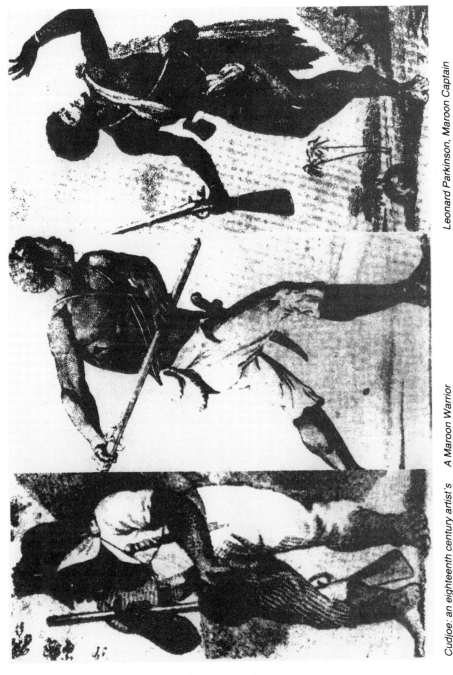

Cudjoe: an eighteenth century artist's impression   A Maroon Warrior   Leonard Parkinson, Maroon Captain

Marcus Garvey, D.C.L. in robe as President General Universal Negro Improvement Association

TRADE UNIONIST

WHEN Marcus was twenty years old he led a printers' strike in a Kingston printery (P.A. Benjamin Printery), where he worked as a Foreman Printer. When his co-workers at the Printery formed the Printers Union and elected to go on strike, young Marcus had already joined the Union, and they selected him as Strike Leader. This was an unusual position, for it's always expected that foremen will take the side of the employers. Young Marcus contradicted that custom and was fired.

From Garvey's early experiences in Kingston, he became known around Jamaica as a Social Worker, a Preacher of the poor and dispossessed and a spokesman for the black working class in Jamaica and the Caribbean.

GARVEY AND COSTA RICA

IN 1910 Garvey left Jamaica for Costa Rica. In Costa Rica he met a maternal uncle who obtained a job for him on one of the United Fruit Company sugar-cane plantations as a time-keeper.

Garvey didn't stay with that job too long. He later obtained work at Port Lim'on — a Caribbean sea port where many West Indians lived. Sometime later he started a newspaper which he called La Nacion — The Nation. This newspaper was used as a medium to organize the West Indian immigrants. The Costa Rica authorities didn't take this too kindly and started showing Marcus hostility. He later left Costa Rica and travelled to other Central American countries such as Nicaragua, Guatemala, Panama, Chile, Ecuador and Peru.

GARVEY'S ARRIVAL IN BRITAIN

IN 1912 Garvey arrived in England. In England he obtained employment on the docks, in seaport cities such as London, Liverpool and Hull.

He later travelled to other European countries, such as France, Germany, Italy, Spain, Austria and Hungary.

In Europe, Marcus didn't publish any newspapers, but he wrote for black Journals, and attended lectures in Law at Birkbeck College in London.

U.N.I.A. FOUNDED

ON July 14th, 1914, Garvey arrived in Jamaica after a long tour, which had taken him through Central America and Europe. Five days later on July 19th, 1914, Marcus Moziah Garvey founded the largest independent black organisation the world has ever known or seen — the Universal Negro Improvement Association (U.N.I.A.).

Garvey became the first President General of the U.N.I.A.

Garvey built the U.N.I.A. so that it became the mouthpiece of black men, women and children the world over.

The U.N.I.A. had branches in every Caribbean island. In Trinidad and Tobago, it's said that Garvey had one of the largest following. There were at least 30 U.N.I.A. Chapters in that island. For the Trinidad Workingmen's Association was affiliated to the U.N.I.A.

GARVEY'S US DEPARTURE

IN the year 1916, Garvey left Jamaica for the United States of America on a lecture tour. In the USA Garvey began organising meetings and preaching to the black community.

NEGRO WORLD NEWSPAPER FOUNDED

GARVEY started a newspaper in 1918 which he called the Negro World. The motto of this newspaper was derived from Garvey's black nationalist cry — 'One God, One Aim, One Destiny.'

THE BLACK STARLINE

THE year 1919 was a most significant year for Garvey and the U.N.I.A. This was so because in 1919 the Black Starline — a steamship company was formed by Garvey's U.N.I.A. as a means of linking the black peoples living outside Africa with Africa. Garvey held a vision that Africa was the rightful place for all Africans to live. Hence, he advocated "Africa for the Africans, those at home, those abroad". The first ship which was acquired was called Yarmouth, but it was later renamed the Frederick Douglass, in honour of the 19th century Black American leader.

The second ship was acquired in April 1920, and it was called Shadyside.

The third ship was called Kenawha, and it was renamed Antonio Maceo — after a Cuban black general who fought for Cuba's independence.

Garvey addressing a crowd at Limon, Costa Rica in 1921

INCORPORATED UNDER THE LAWS OF THE STATE OF DELAWARE

BLACK STAR LINE, INC.

CAPITAL STOCK $10,000,000

SHARES $5. EACH

Shares _____

No. _____

This Certifies

_____ is the owner of

_____ Shares of The Capital Stock of

BLACK STAR LINE, INC. full paid and non-assessable

transferable only on the books of this Corporation in person or by Attorney
upon surrender of this Certificate properly endorsed

IN WITNESS WHEREOF __ said Corporation has caused this Certificate to be
signed by its duly authorized officers and to be sealed with the Seal of the Corporation
this _____ day of _____ A.D. 19___

President

Secretary

THE U.N.I.A. INTERNATIONAL CONVENTION

IN 1920 Marcus Garvey convened the first International Convention of the U.N.I.A. in New York City.

At this Convention, tens of thousands of the U.N.I.A. followers and members marched through the streets of Harlem in colourful uniforms behind their spiritual leader, philosopher and prophet — the invincible Marcus Moziah Garvey.

In a major session of this Convention held in Madison Square Garden, he was quoted as saying that:

"We are the descendants of a people determined to suffer no longer".

THE U.N.I.A. ANTHEM INTERNATIONAL

The anthem of the U.N.I.A. International was:

Ethiopia thou land of our fathers,
Thou land where the Gods loved to be,
As storm cloud at night suddenly gathers
Our armies come rushing to thee
We must in the fight be victorious
When sounds are thrust outward to gleam
For us the victory be glorious
When led by the red, black and green

Chorus:
Advance, Advance to victory
Let Africa be free;
Advance to meet the foe
With the might
Of the red, black and the green.

Ethiopia, the tyrant's falling
Who smote thee upon thy knees
And they children are lustily calling
From over the distant seas.
Jehovah, the great one has heard us,
Has noted our sighs and our tears
With His spirit of love he has stirred us
To be one through the coming years.

Chorus: Advance, advance, etc.

Oh Jehovah, thou God of the ages
Grant unto our sons that lead;
The wisdom Thou gave to Thy sages
When Israel was sore in need.
Thy voice thro the dim past has spoken
Ethiopia shall stretch forth her hand
By Thee shall all fetters be broken
And Heav'ns bless our dear fatherland.

Chorus: Advance, advance, etc.

THE U.N.I.A. FLAG

THE colours of the U.N.I.A. flag were red, black and green.

OTHER U.N.I.A. CONVENTIONS

THE U.N.I.A. held a total of eight conventions — two of these conventions took place in Kingston, Jamaica in 1929 and 1934, five were held in the USA in 1920, 1921, 1922, 1924 and 1926, and the final one was held in Toronto, Canada in 1938.

U.N.I.A. AND THE LEAGUE OF NATIONS

THE League of Nations was the international organisation which preceded the United Nations. The League of Nations was set up in 1919 right after the end of World War I — 1914-1918.

The U.N.I.A made several representations at the League in an effort to seek the decolonializing of all Germany's African colonies, which were taken away from her by the victorious ally nations after World War I. Garvey sought through the U.N.I.A. to have the African colonies handed over to black independent rule.

The first attempt by the U.N.I.A. to lobby for the decolonization of these colonies was made in 1919 at the Paris Peace Conference. This was followed by other representations to the League in 1922, 1923, 1928 and 1931. On the two latter occasions Garvey himself put forward the views of the U.N.I.A., but unfortunately the League of Nations never accepted his proposals.

S.S. Kanawha renamed S.S. Antonio Maceo. This boat was purchased for $160,000.00 and fitted at a cost of over $25,000.00 and later wrecked by an undisciplined crew and by arranged plots

S.S. Yarmouth renamed S.S. Frederick Douglas, merchant flagship of the Black Starline, purchased for $165,000.00

Marcus Garvey, Founder and President General of the
Universal Negro Improvement Association

ATTEMPTED ASSASSINATION

SOMETIME in October, 1919, a man named George Taylor walked into the U.N.I.A. Office seeking to meet Marcus Garvey. When Marcus appeared, and they began conversing, the man pulled out a pistol and fired four shots, two of which hit Garvey — one in his head and the other in the leg. Garvey was rushed to the Harlem Hospital, where he was treated for minor injuries and discharged.

His would be assassin was imprisoned, but died in jail, under strange circumstances, before the court could have known why he attempted to take the life of the great philosopher.

MARCUS'S MARRIAGE, DIVORCE, MARRIAGE

GARVEY's first marriage was to a young Jamaican girl — Amy Ashwood, who was a U.N.I.A. activist. He married her on December 25th 1919, in Liberty Hall, Harlem. Garvey's first association with young Amy Ashwood began in Jamaica, in 1914. However, their marriage did not last too long. It came to an end less than twenty two months after their wedding. On divorcing Amy Ashwood in June 1922, while she was away in England, he married another U.N.I.A. woman activist also named Amy — Amy Jacques in July 1922.

This latter marriage to Amy Jacques lasted until Marcus departed this life in 1940.

STARLINE'S BANKRUPTCY

IN 1923, the Black Starline was forced into bankruptcy mainly because there was a lack of proper managerial skills; along with a high degree of dishonesty by both black and white employees.

It was said that those persons who were assigned the responsibility to negotiate for the fleet of ships, defrauded the company of thousands of dollars. In addition, the white officers quietly sabotaged the line's operation by deliberately wrecking the ship's engines, therefore causing thousands of dollars to be spent on unnecessary repairs.

GARVEY AND LIBERIA

SOON before Emancipation of Slavery in the United States of America, Liberia was established as an African colony in 1820. It was set up as an area mainly for African-American ex-slaves who wanted to re-settle in their native African homeland after they had obtained emancipation.

In 1920, the U.N.I.A. attempted to establish a black colony in Liberia. This was intended to facilitate all Africans living in the Americas, Europe and the Caribbean who were interested in migrating to Africa.

The move to re-establish a link with Liberia came to a halt in 1924, soon after a high-powered U.N.I.A. delegation made an official visit to that country.

The government of Liberia put a stop to the U.N.I.A. plans although a U.N.I.A. sawmill along with other costly equipment were on the way to Liberia. As a result of this abrupt halt to the U.N.I.A. plans to establish links with Liberia, thousands of dollars were again lost by this organization.

GARVEY IMPRISONED

IN 1923, the Federal Court in the USA imprisoned Garvey for mail fraud and tax evasion. He was sentenced to five years at the Atlanta State Prisons by Judge Julian Mack. He eventually obtained bail. But he began his jail sentence in 1925.

GARVEY FREED

IN November 1927 Garvey's prison term was commuted by President Calvin Coolidge.

On his release from prison, Garvey was immediately deported to Jamaica via Panama.

From Panama, Garvey or the Black Messiah as he was sometimes called by his followers, arranged to return to his native Jamaica, where he revived the U.N.I.A.

MARCUS GARVEY — THE POET

YOU AND ME
October 1927 — (Taken from the Negro World)

When we think of all the care
That made life's burden great,
We long for the passing year
To close our sad book of fate:
But if we could stop a while,
And think once the other way,
Life would be just all a smile,
As we go on day by day.

A group of women of the African Motor Corps on parade in New York during the convention of 1925

Members of the Garvey Militia, New York, 1921

Amy Jacques Garvey

We should never make a day night
For to darken life's good view;
Round that turning is the light
That shines as a guide to you;

Think of all that's really good,
Then make it your daily rule;
Smile with Nature's Brotherhood
And none make your footstool

A proverb for every day
And one more for each good night,
Should make life so pleasant, yea,
Would lead us to live all right:
Turn not from sane rectitude,
But make life just like a song;
Go ye not with the multitude,
To any path that's wholly wrong.

GARVEY FORERUNNER OF EMPEROR SELASSIE OF ETHIOPIA

ONE Sunday in 1927, Marcus Garvey prophesied in one of his sermons:

"Look to Africa, where a black King shall be crowned, for the day of deliverance is here".

And when on November 2nd, 1930, Ras Tafari Makonnen, also known to the world as Emperor Selassie I was crowned the 225th Monarch of Ethiopia in a lineage which some historians traced to the union of the Queen Makada of Sheba and Solomon. Most Black Jamaicans claimed that Garvey was indeed some kind of modern-day apostle or prophet.

EUROPEAN TOUR

GARVEY and his wife Amy travelled to Europe, Canada and the Bahamas on an extensive lecture tour in 1928. On this tour he came in contact with a young African student studying in London — Jomo Kenyatta. Kenyatta later became the first President of independent Kenya.

THE BLACKMAN NEWSPAPER

IN early 1929, Marcus started another newspaper which he called The Blackman. The Blackman became the mouthpiece of all black men and women in and out of Jamaica.

THE FORMATION OF GARVEY'S POLITICAL PARTY

SOON after the U.N.I.A.'s sixth international convention which lasted from August 1st-August 31st, 1929, Marcus Garvey launched the first modern political party in the history of the British Caribbean. The name of Garvey's Party was the People's Political Party (P.P.P.).

The P.P.P. was formed in time to participate in the Legislative Council election which was scheduled for late January, 1930.

GARVEY CHARGED AND IMPRISONED

IN September 1929, during his election campaign, Garvey was charged for gross contempt.

Garvey was brought before the Jamaica court where the Judges sentenced him to three months in the St Catherine District Prison along with a fine of one hundred pounds. This sentence put a halt to his Legislative Council Campaign.

This prison term didn't deter or silence Marcus. He eventually took part in another set of elections i.e. the Kingston and St Andrews Corporation (K.S.A.C.) Council elections which was soon due. Garvey entered this election as a candidate, while campaigning from inside prison. He won the seat for Ward No 3. On release from prison he attended three meetings of the K.S.A.C. Council. Some of the members of the Council attempted to unseat him on a technicality, that he had missed three consecutive meetings of the Council while he was imprisoned. The seat was declared vacant, and a by-election held. Marcus eventually re-won the seat unopposed.

The K.S.A.C. was eventually closed down by the colonial authorities in September 1930. And when they re-opened it in 1931, Marcus remained as a member of that Council. While serving as a K.S.A.C. Council member, Garvey also fought a bitter struggle for the acceptance of an eight hour day and a minimum wage for all Council workers. This battle was never won.

THE 1934 CONVENTION

IN 1934, the U.N.I.A. held its seventh International Convention. At this Convention, the U.N.I.A. Delegates present agreed with a proposed five year plan of the U.N.I.A. to reorganise itself. In addition, the Convention also sanctioned the idea for Marcus Garvey to move his operations to London. It was generally agreed by delegates, that if Garvey was made to operate from a major world capital, the problems of bringing together the fragments of the U.N.I.A. should be solved easier.

Marcus Garvey and family

Part of a large crowd at Garvey's deportation

GARVEY'S DEPARTURE TO LONDON

MARCUS Moziah Garvey left Kingston, Jamaica, for the United Kingdom in April 1935 for the last time. He never again put his foot on Jamaican soil.

LAST U.N.I.A. CONVENTION

IN August 1938, the U.N.I.A. under Marcus Garvey held its eighth and final convention in Toronto, Canada.

FINAL CARIBBEAN TOUR

SOMETIME in 1937, Garvey visited a series of Caribbean islands, among them were Trinidad and Tobago, Guyana, Dominica, St Lucia, St Vincent, Barbados, Antigua. But his ship did not stop at Kingston, Jamaica. It was said that everywhere he stopped, he had large cheerful crowds gathering around to hear his messages and speeches.

In Trinidad, the authorities attempted to debar him from entering the island, but because of Deputy Mayor, Captain Arthur Cipriani who came to his assistance, he was eventually given permission to land.

GARVEY DEPARTED

ON June 10th 1940, the man, Marcus Moziah Garvey, died from a stroke in England, without ever setting foot on the African continent. When Garvey died he was approaching his fifty-third birthday.

GARVEY PROCLAIMED

IN 1964, Garvey was proclaimed a National Hero of Jamaica (O.N.H.), therefore becoming Jamaica's first National Hero.

GARVEY RESPONSIBLE FOR TWO MOVEMENTS

OUT of the doctrine and Black nationalist philosophy of Marcus Moziah Garvey, two famous movements developed in the Western World. 1. The Black Muslim i.e. The Nation of Islam emerged during the late 1930s in the United States of America, led by a former corporal of the U.N.I.A. — Elijah Muhammad; and 2. The Rastafari Movement developed in Jamaica around the time of the Coronation of Emperor Tafari — Selassie I. The Rastafari Movement has now grown in large proportions to include every island in the Caribbean, Europe, the Americas and the African Continent.

Therefore Garvey lives in these movements.

30

Garvey being taken by Federal Marshals to the Tomb's Prison, New York

Garvey delivers a stirring farewell address minutes before deportation at New Orleans, 1927

EXCERPTS FROM GARVEY'S FAREWELL ADDRESS

IN 1925 after being sentenced to serve five years in the Atlanta State Prison, Garvey wrote to his followers:

"If I die in Atlanta my work shall then only begin, but I shall live in the physical or spiritual to see the day of Africa's glory. When I am dead wrap the mantle of the Red, Black and Green around me, for in the new life I shall rise with God's grace and blessing to lead the millions up the heights of triumph with the colours that you well know. Look for me in the whirlwind or the storm, look for me all around you, for with God's grace, I shall come and bring with me countless millions of black slaves who have died in America and the West Indies and the millions in Africa to aid you in the fight for Liberty, Freedom and Life".

MARCUS MOZIAH GARVEY — PAN AFRICAN GIANT

THE philosophy and opinions of Marcus Moziah Garvey have been analysed in great depth by many writers and historians, both past and present. However, many analysts of the Garvey movement have looked upon it mainly from the viewpoint that one of his greatest achievements was the organising of the Universal Negro Improvement Association (U.N.I.A.) which he founded in 1914.

But many historians and writers have failed to see that one of his greatest accomplishments besides organising the large masses of Africans throughout the world into one organisation, or the publishing of literature in the form of the Blackman or the Nation Newspapers, was the creation of the Black Starline Steamship Company.

Now I am not indicating or advocating that any of Garvey's achievements in bringing the African race together were superior to any other. Though it must be observed that so often we hear the critics saying or writing that the U.N.I.A. Black Starline Steamship Company was a complete failure. It was the financial bankruptcy of this company which caused the United States Government after continued instigation from intellectuals such as Dr Dubois, that led up to Garvey's arrest in 1923 for mail fraud in the USA and to his eventual deportation in 1927 from that country.

If Garvey's Black Starline expedition failed, it did so because the might of America was against it succeeding. The United States Government went as far as to communicate with the Government of Liberia with whom they knew officials of the U.N.I.A. had been in contact. The United States Government informed the Liberian Government that they should abandon any sort of assistance or trade arrangements with Garvey's movement.

In addition, at that time there were not many African pilots trained in sea navigation, therefore, the Black Starline had to rely heavily on recruiting European trained officers to direct the company's fleet of ships. It is now obvious that sabotage was inevitable by both African traitors who were employed along with the white members of staff.

The main aim of the Black Starline Company was to put in practice the very crucial slogan of the U.N.I.A. —

"Africa for the Africans, those home, those abroad."

Indeed, such a statement by Garvey in the 1920s would have surely put fear into the hearts of the European ruling class. Because its implementation meant that, if all or most of the Africans who were transplanted or born in the West decided to leave the colonies, the colonies would be meaningless, and capitalism would be useless. This was due to the fact that a large section of the labouring or down-presed peoples who comprised the population in the Caribbean, America or even Europe were of African origin.

The result of an exodus being implemented meant no labour force to man the capitalist factories and industries in the USA or to work on the docks or waterfronts in the Caribbean, Liverpool and other ports in Britain.

Even today, "Africa for the Africans" should still have deep and consequential meaning, that is why though Garvey was not a formally educated person by way of university training, he remains the greatest organiser of the African race in the twentieth century, and probably for centuries to follow.

Garvey was a Pan-African Giant and he knew that a people without a land base and knowledge of themselves are a lost people, that is why he emphasised,

"No man should give up a continent for an island,"

and he declared,

"Just as a tree without roots is dead, so a people without a history and cultural roots becomes a dead people".

As Africans living in the Western World, it is very important to remember that Africa is all that we have, that is why we must defend it, and fight for its total freedom and unification under a just and equitable political and social system where there would not exist any form of exploitation of man by man.

Garvey supervising a U.N.I.A. Parade

During the 1920s Marcus Garvey was able to sell millions of shares in the Black Starline. Many of our parents and grandparents were willing to make the sacrifice in order to forward home to Africa. For chattel slavery had only come to an end in the English speaking Caribbean less than a century or so, and Garvey was well aware of the plight of our people in that period .

Many Africans, i.e. both men and women, were still suffering from inferior-superior complexes which were institutionalised by slavery. Furthermore, although slavery was said to be abolished in 1834 in the British Caribbean and 1865 in the United States, not many African folks were privileged to be educated.

In the period after slavery, education was a privilege mainly for the planter and ruling classes. The bulk of the African population were involved in trades as artisans, working as carpenters, plumbers, masons, tailors etc. It was only a few like Dr W E Dubois who were able to make it to university level. It is not surprising that those intellectuals such as Dubois were the ones who misunderstood Garvey and misinterpreted what he preached.

However, in the new development of Pan-Africanism as a concept and philosophy to scientifically guide our people, Garveyism, its ideas and opinions must be acknowledged. Because, if there were no Marcus Garvey, then there would not have been an Elijah Muhammad or a Nation of Islam, and there would not have been a Dr Martin Luther King Junior, a Malcolm X or a Kwame Toure (i.e. Stokely Carmichael) to expound on Black Power and Pan Africanism. If there were no Garvey, who would have been the forerunner to the Ras Tafari movement?

The man Marcus Mosiah Garvey was and still is a fine and exemplary African man, who lived and would continue to live for the development and unification of all Africa and her peoples. Garvey knew that unless our people became organised into an international organisation with a land base on the continent of Africa, we, as a people, would not obtain and command any respect.

In his role as organiser, he proved to be a general on the field, creating organ after organ, i.e. from *The Nation* to *The Blackman* newspapers, to ensure that our peoples wherever they resided, received the message, so that they could renew their dignity and self pride, in order that one day we might eventually rise up from our deep slumber and help free Africa's children.

Therefore, as a profound leader one can say without any doubts that Marcus Moziah Garvey is the father of modern day Pan-Africanism.

INTERNATIONAL CONVENTION OF NEGROES OF THE WORLD

U.N.I.A. Convention bringing Africans together from around the world

Gathering of U.N.I.A. activists at Liberty Hall 1921

African Fundamentalism

A Racial Hierarchy and Empire for Negroes

NEGRO'S FAITH *must be* CONFIDENCE IN SELF

His Creed: ONE GOD ❧ ONE AIM ❧ ONE DESTINY

The time has come for the Negro to forget and cast behind him his hero worship and adoration of other races, and to start out immediately to create and emulate heroes of his own. We must canonize our own saints, create our own martyrs, and elevate to positions of fame and honor black men and women who have made their distinct contributions to our racial history. Sojourner Truth is worthy of the place of sainthood alongside of Joan of Arc; Crispus Attucks and George William Gordon are entitled to the halo of martyrdom with no less glory than that of the martyrs of any other race. Toussaint L'Ouverture's brilliancy as a soldier and statesman outshone that of a Cromwell, Napoleon and Washington; hence, he is entitled to the highest place as a hero among men. Africa has produced countless numbers of men and women, in war and in peace, whose lustre and bravery outshine that of any other people. Then why not see good and perfection in ourselves? We must inspire a literature and promulgate a doctrine of our own without any apologies to the powers that be. The right is ours and God's. Let contrary sentiment and cross opinions go to the winds. Opposition to race independence is the weapon of the enemy to defeat the hope of an unfortunate people. We are entitled to our own opinions and not obligated to or bound by the opinions of others.

A Peep at the Past

If others laugh at you, return the laughter to them; if they mimic you, return the compliment with equal force. They have no more right to dishonor, disrespect and disregard your feeling and manhood than you have in dealing with them. Honor them when they honor you, disrespect and disregard them when they vilely treat you. Their arrogance is but skin deep and an assumption that has no foundation in morals or in law. They have sprung from the same family tree of obscurity as we have; their history is as rude in its primitiveness as ours; their ancestors ran wild and naked, lived in caves and in branches of trees, like monkeys, as ours; they made human sacrifices, ate the flesh of their own dead and the raw meat of the wild beast for centuries even as they accuse us of doing; their cannibalism was more prolonged than ours; when we were embracing the arts and sciences on the banks of the Nile their ancestors were still drinking human blood and eating out of the skulls of their conquered dead; when our civilization had reached the noon day of progress they were still running naked and sleeping in holes and caves with rats, bats and other insects and animals. After we had already unfathomed the mystery of the stars and reduced the heavenly constellations to minute and regular calculus they were still backwoodsmen, living in ignorance and blatant darkness.

Why Be Discouraged?

The world today is indebted to us for the benefits of civilization. They stole our arts and sciences from Africa. Then why should we be ashamed of ourselves? Their *modern improvements* are but *duplicates* of a grander civilization that we reflected thousands of years ago, without the advantage of what is buried and still hidden, to be resurrected and reintroduced by the intelligence of our generation and our posterity. Why should we be discouraged because somebody laughs at us today? Who can tell what tomorrow will bring forth? Did they not laugh at Moses, Christ and Mohammed? Was there not a Carthage, Greece and Rome? We see and have changes every day, so pray, work, be steadfast and be not dismayed.

Nothing Must Kill the Empire Urge

As the Jew is held together by his *religion*, the white races by the assumption and the unwritten law of *superiority*, and the Mongolian by the precious tie of *blood*, so likewise the Negro must be united in one *grand racial hierarchy*. Our union must know no *clime, boundary* or *nationality*. Like the great Church of Rome, Negroes the world over *must practice one faith*, that of Confidence in themselves, with One God! One Aim! One Destiny! Let no religious scruples, no political machination divide us, but let us hold together under all climes and in every country, making among ourselves a Racial Empire upon which "the sun shall never set."

Allegiance to Self First

Let no voice but your own speak to you from the depths. Let no influence but your own rouse you in time of peace and time of war. Hear all, but attend only to that which concerns you. Your allegiance shall be to your God, then to your family, race and country. Remember always that the Jew in his political and economic urge is always first a Jew; the white man is first a white man under all circumstances, and you can do no less than being first and always a Negro, and then all else will take care of itself. Let no one inoculate you with evil doctrines to suit their own conveniences. There is no humanity before that which starts with yourself. "Charity begins at home." First to thyself be true, and "thou canst not then be false to any man."

We are Arbiters of Our Own Destiny

God and Nature first made us what we are, and then out of our own creative genius we make ourselves what we want to be. Follow always that great law. Let the sky and God be our limit, and Eternity our measurement. There is no height to which we cannot climb by using the active intelligence of our own minds. Mind creates, and as much as we desire in Nature we can have through the creation of our own minds. Being at present the scientifically weaker race, you shall treat others as they treat you, but in your homes and everywhere possible you must teach the higher development of science to your children, and be sure to develop a race of scientists par excellence, for in science and religion lies our only hope to withstand the designs of modern materialism. Never forget your God. Remember, we live, work and pray for the establishing of a great and binding *racial hierarchy*, the founding of a *racial empire* whose only natural, spiritual and political limits shall be God and Africa, at home and abroad.

Marcus Garvey

QUOTABLE QUOTATIONS FROM MARCUS MOSIAH GARVEY

"There is nothing in the world common to man, that man cannot do."

"The ends you serve that are selfish will take you no further than yourself, but the ends you serve that are for all in common will take you even into eternity."

"Admiration is a form of appreciation that is sometimes mistaken for something else. There may be something about you that suggests good fellowship when kept at a distance, but in closer contact would not be tolerated, otherwise it be love."

"Wake up Ethiopia! Wake up Africa! Let us work towards the one glorious end of a free, redeemed and mighty nation. Let Africa be a bright star among the constellation of nations."

"This is the day of racial activity, when each and every group of this great human family must exercise its own initiative and influence in its own protection, therefore, Africans should be more determined today than they have ever been because the mighty forces of the world are operating against non-organized groups of people, who are not ambitious enough to protect their own interests."

"A man's bread and butter is only insured when he works for it."

"The only protection against Injustice in man is power — physical, financial and scientific."

"The masses make the nation and the race. If the masses are illiterate, that is the judgement passed on the race by those who are critical of its existence."

"Education is the medium by which a people are prepared for the creation of their own particular civilization, and the advancement and glory of their own race."

"Nationhood is the only means by which modern civilization can completely protect itself."

"Nationhood is the highest ideal of all peoples."

"Let Africa be our guiding star — our star of destiny."

"So many of us find excuses to get out of the African Race, because we are led to believe that the race is unworthy — that it has not accomplished anything. Cowards that we are! It is we who are unworthy, because we are not contributing to the uplift and up-building of this noble race."

"Be as proud of your race today as our fathers were in the days of yore. We have a beautiful history, and we shall create another in the future that will astonish the world."

Woman
"What the night is to the day, is woman to man. The period of change that brings us light out of darkness, darkness out of light, and semi-light out of darkness are like the changes we find in woman day to day.

She makes one happy, then miserable. You are the kind, then unkind. Constant yet inconstant. Thus we have woman. No real man can do without her."

"Peoples everywhere are travelling toward industrial opportunities and greater political freedom. As a race oppressed, it is for us to prepare ourselves that at any time the great change in industrial freedom and political liberty comes about, we may be able to enter into the new era as partakers of the joys to be inherited."

"All peoples are struggling to blast a way through the industrial monopoly of races and nations, but the African as a whole has failed to grasp its true significance and seems to delight in filling only that place created for him by the white man."

"No race in the world is so just as to give others, for the asking, a square deal in things economic, political and social."

"Men who are in earnest are not afraid of consequences."

"No one knows when the hour of Africa's Redemption cometh. It is in the wind. It is coming. One day, like a storm, it will be here. When that day comes all Africa will stand together."

"Any sane man, race or nation that desires freedom must first of all think in terms of blood. Why, even the Heavenly Father tells us that 'without the shedding of blood there can be no remission of sins.' Then how in the name of God, with history before us, do we expect to redeem Africa without preparing ourselves — some of us to die."

"Every man has a right to his own opinion. Every race has a right to its own action; therefore let no man persuade you against your will, let no other race influence you against your own."

"The greatest weapon used against Africa is Disorganization."

"If you have no confidence in self you are twice defeated in the race of life. With confidence you have won even before you have started."

"At no time within the last five hundred years can one point to a single instance of the African as a race of haters."

"The African has loved even under severest punishment. In slavery the African loved his master, he safeguarded his home even when he further planned to enslave him. We are not a race of Haters, but Lovers of humanity's cause."

"There can be no peace among men and nations, so long as the strong continues to oppress the weak, so long as injustice is done to other peoples, just so long will we have cause for war, and make a lasting peace an impossibility."

"Hungry men have no respect for law, authority or human life."

"The battles of the future, whether they be physical or mental, will be fought on scientific lines, and the race that is able to produce the highest scientific development, is the race that will ultimately rule."

"Let us prepare today. For the Tomorrow in the lives of the nations will be so eventful that Africans everywhere will be called upon to play their part in the survival of the fittest human group."

"Day by day we hear the cry of 'Africa for the Africans'. This cry has become a positive determined one. It is a cry that is raised simultaneously the world over, because of the universal oppression that affects the African."

"We want to see the black man highly developed, seeking to discover the hidden forces in nature, harnessing them to his will for the good fo all."

PS RESEARCH ASSOCIATES SCHOOL TIMES PUBLICATIONS has refrained from usage of the term 'Negro' as used by Garvey, and instead has replaced it with the word African. This is not a form of disrespect to Garvey or his U.N.I.A. but we simply think that 'Negro' is a demeaning word.

H.I.M.

ግርማዊ ፡ ቀዳማዊ ፡ ኃይለ ፡ ሥላሴ ፡ ንጉሠ ፡ ነገሥት ፡ ዘኢትዮጵያ ።

42

IMPORTANT DATES OF HISTORICAL EVENTS

	1776	The American Revolution
	1789	The French Revolution
	1791	The Haitian Revolution — Haiti became the First Black Republic
August 1st	1834	Emancipation of Africans enslaved in the Caribbean
	1840	Marx's 'socialist' ideology awakens Europe
	1845	Start of East Indian Indentureship
	1865	Slavery abolished in the USA
August 17th	1887	Birth of Marcus Mosiah Garvey, St Anns, Jamaica
July 23rd	1889	Birth of Ras Tafari — Emperor Haile Selassie, in Ethiopia
	1899	Tobago was made a ward of Trinidad
	1914	World War I starts
	1919	Waterfront Riots, Trinidad
	1925	Limited Adult Franchise granted to the people of Trinidad and Tobago
November 2nd	1930	The Coronation of the 225th and final Emperor to the Ethiopian Throne — Emperor Haile Selassie 1
	1937	Labour unrest in the T & T Oilfields led by Tubal Uriah 'Buzz' Butler
	1939	World War II commences
	1940	Marcus Garvey died in England
	1945	End of World War II
	1946	Full Adult Franchise granted to the people of Trinidad and Tobago
	1950	The Butler Party is the first Party to contest Trinidad and Tobago elections
	1956	Peoples National Movement (PNM) became the first Party Government in Trinidad and Tobago
	1958	Federation was formed among 10 British colonies in the Caribbean. The capital was Trinidad.
	1959	The Cuban Revolution led by Dr Fidel Castro
	1961	Federation was dissolved
August 6th	1962	Jamaica became independent
August 31st	1962	Trinidad and Tobago became independent
May 24th	1963	Organisation of African Unity (OAU) formed
May 26th	1966	Guyana achieved independence
	1968	CARIFTA was formed
Febrruay	1970	Social and political unrest in Trinidad and Tobago led by the National Joint Action Committee
	1973	CARICOM was formulated (CARIFTA dissolved)
September 13th	1973	Beverly Jones of the National United Freedom Fighters was killed by a combined Police-Army Unit in Trinidad

September 24th	1976	Trinidad and Tobago became a Republic within the Commonwealth
March 13th	1979	The New Jewel Movement led by Maurice Bishop seized political power in Grenada. It was the first overthrow in the English speaking Caribbean
March 29th	1981	The death of the first Prime Minister of Trinidad and Tobago — Dr Eric Eustace Williams
October 19th	1983	Maurice Bishop, popular Prime Minister of the People's Revolutionary Government (PRG) was assassinated in Fort Rupert, St Georges, Grenada
October 25th	1983	US President Ronald Reagan instructs US Marines and other Caribbean military forces to invade the 90 square miles island of Grenada

Compiled by Seko Tafari and W W Hislop for Research Associates School Times Publications.

RAPSO FAREWELL — AN ODE FOR GARVEY

Marcus Garvey, Marcus Garvey,
Freedom Fighter and Friend
Lover of African peoples
To your very end.
I can see you Garvey
De Black Starliner is sailing
I hear your voice rumbling .....
rumbling in de whirlwind.
Your message is spreading
Manifesting in Rastafari,
Echoing Black Power
Black Power! Beyond the Carib Sea
and Blue Mountain region
From St Ann's Jamaica
Harlem and Brixton.
East Dry River to Trench Town.
Oh Garvey! Oh Garvey!
I hear you saying
"Africa for all Africans"
Remember your pride and liberty.
Oh Garvey! Oh Garvey!
We bid you farewell
Lead us in dis struggle
Oh Gosh! To de very end.

Seko Tafari

SOME SUGGESTIONS FOR FURTHER READING

Martin, Tony, *Marcus Garvey, Hero* No 3. The New Marcus Garvey Library — a Majority Press publication

Cass, Frank, *Philosophy and Opinions of Marcus Garvey*

Martin, Tony, *The Poetical Works of Marcus Garvey* No 2. The New Marcus Garvey Library — a Majority Press publication

Clarke, John Henrik, *Marcus Garvey and the Vision of Africa*. New York. Random House, 1974

Garvey, Amy Jacques, *Garvey and Garveyism*, New York. Collier Books, 1970